STREETS THAT SPEAK

STREETS THAT SPEAK
Streets That Do Not Have Enough
and
Streets That Do Have Enough

Charles Holmes

Streets That Speak

Copyright © 2018 Charles Holmes

Printed in the United States of America

Published by

Big Hat Press
Lafayette, California
www.bighatpress.com

DEDICATED TO

Rosalie Louise Gallick
Charles John Holmes Sr.
Aidan Lee Elenteny

BOOKS BY CHARLES HOLMES

POETRY BOOKS

Streets That Speak*
For Understanding Eyes
Reflections of the Heart
Reflections of the Soul

*About streets that do not have enough and streets that do have enough

NON-FICTION BOOKS

Hard Life, Kindness Ever Awake†
Thoughts From Millie**

**Interview quotes/practical wisdom from an elder at 89, 90, and 91 years old

CHILDREN'S BOOKS

Bo Loney Goes to a New School
The Silver-lettered Poem in the Sky
The Cloth of 100 Wrinkles
Aidan Dreams Amazing Dreams
Aidan Dreams of 105 Fortune Cookies
Kid-like Poetry with a Bit of a Smile...Sometimes
Kid-like Poetry for Kids Who Are "Cool" at School
Kid-like Poetry for Kids Who Like Recess
Shy Kai Wished He Could Fly†

†In process

Available on Amazon
To contact author, please email rlg121212@gmail.com

CONTENTS

STREETS THAT DON'T HAVE ENOUGH

DARK STREETS

DINGY STREETS

DEEP STREETS

FEARFUL STREETS

STREETS THAT DO HAVE ENOUGH

WAKING STREETS

WINDING STREETS

SPACIOUS STREETS

SILENT STREETS

PREAMBLE

CHARLES HOLMES worked in the Tenderloin, perhaps San Francisco's most famous slum, from March 26, 1979 until September 6, 1983, during which time he wrote some of what he had heard and observed. He also spent a summer there (minus two weeks to help at a boy's camp) when 17 years old, a youth alone at Golden Gate and Leavenworth Streets. His "Streets That Do Not Have Enough" come from these two experiences. His "Streets That Do Have Enough" are some poems beyond streets that beg for coin.

Streets That Speak gives a verbal picture of streets with not much protection and others with more blessings. It is written as a reminder of souls with sagging roofs and some no roof at all, and those who fortunately have never held a cardboard sign begging for dollar or morsel, nor have gone to sleep in a tiny, dusty room with noise outside, bathroom down the hall.

The author lays thoughts "on the table," to be picked up should the reader choose to do so. He hopes that his efforts might be a help to look at the bright side.

STREETS THAT DON'T HAVE ENOUGH

DARK STREETS

On a Street in the Tenderloin

Can I love the man who just stands there staring?
>Or do I even notice him enough to care?
>Or do I really see him at all?

Does my glance bring him meaning?
>Or just nervous eyes?

Can I imagine that I might be that man someday?
>And really believe it?

Can I eliminate the thought as an impossibility?
Can I feel what it would be like?
>…is like?

If it (that reality) should be,
>would I love myself as I stand there,
>or at night before I go to sleep,
>when I'm alone and it's dark?

If it (that reality) should be,
>could I accept it?
>…accept it, and say, "That's life."

Accept myself?
If it (that reality) should be,
>could I be glad to see
>the morning sun shine each day?
>…and stand there staring?

A Giving Street Person

The street person told me that his "lady"
      sent him a ticket to fly home to New Jersey
            (from San Francisco).
He was looking forward to it.
      But he was still on the street with his sign,
"Donations for Winos."
      Two friends of mine were parking their car
and didn't have change for the meter.
      Unsolicited, he filled the coin slot,
offering to them an hour of security.
      Who says street people don't give?

On the Street at Night

"The hardest thing is 9:30 p.m. and no one to talk to."

Street People

January 20,1983

Street people were sleeping outside of our Center.
I gave them some yellowish-green bananas.
    They said, "Thank you."
Within a short time, one came into the complex
    asking for a bag in which to put the peels.
He said they didn't want to throw them in the street.
    Upon receiving a container, he nodded, "Thank you."

Who Cares on Any Street?

May 11, 1983

"Who out there cares about me?"
Next question -
do street people care about me?

A Slum at Bedtime

"Everyone goes his own way at night,"
        said the crouched man on the broken sidewalk,
reacting quickly to the point-blank question,
        "WHERE do the destitute sleep?"

7 Year Old Wisdom

The 7 year old with a slight lisp
       started in a new school with children
he had not seen before.
       His crying words,
"They think I'm dumb
       because
they don't know me."

Out There

Pain raced across his ankles bare,
  while his forehead stretched in eloquent age.
Thirty-seven years of walking alone
  had carved a "dance-less" statue
of shaggy skin on silent air.
  But, he roller skates after work now,
with biking speed, wires and all,
  even the ones behind sidewalk trees.
There, the money scream can't be heard,
  clothes don't matter,
nor the lane he's in,
  it's just him and the wind on his face.

Grown Ups Will Do It

The 10 year old looked at the sky.
      Then said,
"The world will soon be dust,
      and grown ups will do it."

Street Sleeper

February 5, 1981

Months of begging, sleeping in alleys.
   He met a social worker who lined up a temporary
   address
and arranged a meeting with a Welfare agency.
   He missed the appointment.

***

His life was hard.
   His crutches helped, but moving was slow.
He said the cheapest room was $14 a night.
   It was beg or the cold alley.
I gave him $5 to add to his $9, and again wrote down
   the social worker's number.
After slowly walking a few blocks with him,
   I decided to make an appointment for him.
But will he go? The last time, "No."
   Will he pull himself together enough to conquer
the insecurity, the exhaustion, lack of nourishment,
   and all the rest…and be there?
Sounds simple, to arrive at an interview which means money
   and a little better life, but after "living on the streets"
nothing is.

***

I found out later that he didn't go.

DINGY STREETS

Panhandler

Does anyone love the man
      begging at corner's edge...?
continually reaching out,
      a few answering in.

Does he have a plan
      for his steps,
one calm amid outer noise,
      hope there somehow?

Does he walk on through
      noontide sun or cruel wind,
feel it's not just another day,
      a mighty note somewhere?

Coffee Shops with Pastry

Coffee shops with pastry.
        What's the attraction?
Is it the coffee or the pastry?
        Or, is it someone to talk to?

It is a place to sit,
        to stop the motion
which could become sickness.

Resting is necessary.
        Prices are not inexpensive,
And for so much caffeine!

Is stopping a reward
        for ruining one's body?
Or an excuse to be less lonely?
        Or, just something to do
with people around.

Singles' Place to Eat

Clouded cigarette smoke rising to still fan on ceiling,
      more pointedly, aloneness,
      basically conversationless isolation.
With dots of commercial and conventional life
      oozing from painted pictures on the walls,
from cash register area,
      the cook's domain,
the bowl containing mixed jellies,
      and colorful table cloth.

The meal, minestrone watered down,
      solid bread with too little butter,
main entree not enough tartar sauce,
      and dry mashed potatoes,
advertised hot plate,
      cold to eyes and to taste.

But the touch of joy,
      customer kissing hand of smiling waitress (twice).
The clear statement, the price,
      the importance of supper with people around.
The emotional cry,
      grim reminder of the loneliness of Sunday night
for the single person…
      the beauty of a pleasant encounter.

You Never Know

You never know
          until you know,
then you are not sure.

A Man Crying

Neurotic, of course.
      Tears of beauty, truth, love, fear...
The big problem,
      too much crying alone.

Thin-faced Time

Do I die before I live, or
        do I live before I die?
Does something die outside of me
        when I die, or
does something inside of me die
        when I live?

Going to Sleep at 84 in the Slums

84,
frail, lacking physical vitality,
     living alone in a violent city.
Time to turn off lights
     and hope for another day.
Fear clings to the door;
     noise seems endless.
Fire could start,
     someone could smash hinges to the floor,
sickness could attack.
     Death could call.
Imagination soars.

"Has the world passed me by?"
     "Have my friends pit me as a failure?"
Past defeats raise their heads,
     black despairs glide from mind to heart,
dark dreads beset, harass, torture…

Going to sleep in raging ghetto
     with its known and unknown sounds…
What is the sure shield
     from the potential terror of the night?

Senior with Social "Security" Looks at Life

Life has gone quickly, but whose hasn't?
Doing it over,
I would not have leaned so much on discouragement's way,
waited so long for perfect certainty before deciding,
reacted to so many "maybe situations",
rumors, gossip, questionable guesses.
Would have depended less on what others thought and said,
accepted myself earlier,
over-reacted less,
been more creative,
"picked up the pieces" better,
created own opportunities more,
worked with less anxiety,
energy level higher,
hopefully seeing alternate ways,
and
tried harder somehow
to have the right people around.

Squalid Streets

Plastic signs on real streets,
      littered, sloppy, peopled,
broken glass, scattered needles,
      a few sidewalk chairs,
occupants almost saying
      "I sit" instead of "I am."
Cup-sippers eyeing graffiti,
      perhaps searching for art.

Do any ask self
      "Am I really what I experience?"

Video Violence

Who was that masked murdered man? Who cares?
      Does the clashing metal have meanings
      for the wingless watcher?
or is it just profligate pleasure seeing bodies assaulted
      amid loud, wild music?
The view seems to become a blotter
      accepting what he knows is not normal
      or necessarily right,
      which for the moment seems to fulfill a need.
He embraces selfishness and a wounded spirit.
      And when silence claims another life,
it's like a gold medal
      and the slender assurance,
      "Yes, but I am OK."

Society/Slum People

Greatness in all - rich, poor, very poor.
  Life in the penthouse, mezzanine, basement.
   What's the difference!

Faces of Street People reveal their bedroom.
  Hands of elite, satin sheets smooth.
   There's a difference!

But, racking pain spinning within.
  Tanned skin not what it appears.
   The other! Throbbing veins transparent.

Yet, ambiguous eyes, sickly ears, twisted tongues.
  Unhealed wounds, urban nights, cancerous sun.
   All find their victims, whatsoever the
   fashions.

Empty loneliness, the gestalt of it all.
    Just much-used ports.
        Strangely wrangled coarse-weed clinging.

Confusion's final run, ever the same!
    The undefined longing for ultimate meaning.
        Childish desire to see again morning light.

Life…rags, bronze or golden threads.
    A fleeting instant of fear-love in eternity.
        Whatever! The solitary drive…
            A wintry heart weathering.

DEEP STREETS

Tenderloin Kids Playing, 1979

Children in school yard,
      skating, falling, resting,
laughing, hitting, running, throwing,
      kicking, dodging.

So unaware of life, perhaps so aware of it.
      Happy to be alive,
appreciative of the moment,
      wrapped up in Now.

So unconcerned about supper,
      night's rest, day's work.
So conscious of play, where they are.
      They are children,
determined to enjoy TODAY.

From the Curb Looking Down

How few deep relationships in life…Why?
      Perhaps because of
the difficulty of embracing the unacceptable part of me,
      not going with enough the unacceptable part of others,
not loving self sufficiently,
      desiring too much, or too little,
unsettled peace inside,
      being fearful and unfree,
not taking sometimes reasonable risks,
      not accepting myself,
not living in the present,
      not trusting the Now situation to pass in a major way,
not really understanding intelligently the connection with death.

Dying Alone

Naked windows drinking in irregular breathing,
      visiting nurses silently think, "It's a hard day."

Visitors stopping to stare at yellow skin,
      faintly mesmerized by toothless gasping.

A knowing family stretching cloth across rail protective,
      with faithful shadows forlorn on crumbled walls.

Long night whispers to still curtains
      with casual coldness,
its unspoken message, "He'll die alone."

A Cat, a Bridge, a Sunset

Clawing cat continually stares
      at well-painted idols on battered bridge.

He bows as he had so often
      missing the sinking sunset again,
lighting of verdant earth
      beneath feline feet.

When he straightens up,
      he sees for the first time
that it was just himself and the span,
      nothing in-between.

Perhaps he realizes then,
      that he could not love the sundown
simply because
      he has never seen it.

"Body Language"

Awakening senses,
     trying to be alert in sweltering afternoon, lonely nights.

Ears, sensitive to trembling trees, rolling hills of straw,
     purring of striped kittens,
       savage dogs ready to pursue at break of leash.
Eyes, staring at adult stone creased by weight-bearing lines,
     angelic beauty of rosy-cheeked smiling baby,
       cracked sidewalks lecturing to stormy sky.
Nostrils, taking in sickening odors from grayish cement,
     questionable incense seeping from moss-covered walls,
       sluggish air hiding uncanny osmotic power.
Hands, callous from hazardous employment,
     extended skin, furrowed, wrinkled,
       quivering in winter cold.
Feet, bruised, halting, tortured, cursed,
     dancing on dilapidated, creaking floor,
       perhaps unconsciously looking for clear window
       with splendid view.
Mouth, hungering for morsels,
     ready silence in devouring sun,
       whispering brokenly, "I tried…I really tried."

Listening

How could it be wrong
        to dream snow castles on sanguine waves,
or playful kittens typing letters on rock ledge
        which overlooks dancing ocean?
Why not visualize vast comic waters,
        arid existence's irrational rush?

        ***

Before it murmurs in ghostly stillness,
        I really do need more sunsets,
sprightly walks in untrodden woods,
        whistling strolls in misty rain,
short runs on broken sidewalks,
        sidelong glances at bobbing boats
in wooden berths.

        ***

The wanderer asks, does life hear its own music?

        ***

It's been a long, hot day.
        Evening is cool,
am I finally learning to listen?

Nuclear-minded Panhandler

Nuclear-time-clock on his lips now and then
      which has helped him to live,
less worry about hanging skin from elbow to armpit,
      falling hair, sagging chin,
little losses, someone who seems to be opposing,
      "security" of his life's way.

Treasures time, calculating risks.
      Does he really want to reach for street's gold rings?
He wonders if there's a nuclear madman out there,
      one who feels little for true life,
twisted mind perhaps desiring stinging revenge.
      His question: how old is he?

Monastic Log

Monastic log on sacred fire,
      calmly pressing center stage,
surrounded by magnetized eyes,
      feeling subtle magic of guarded beauty,
flickering flames feeding purgatorial air,
      crackling blaze hypnotizing deep darkness.

Limelight sparkling awesomely,
      creating flashing aura,
birthing open-mouthed silence,
      melting wakeful senses secretly.

An unpaintable grace,
      luring reaching hand
to a breathing, sleeping, sensual magnet,
      which lives alone, quiet and warm.

Destiny

Still, they worship the golden calf,
       try to kill the first born,
turf, empire, kingdom, whatever the word,
       they must possess, or be forlorn.

They observe the lane for cart pushers,
       not frequent shopping mall.
A gold chain to hang on beguiling neck,
       the hope, "Time and chance for all."

FEARFUL STREETS

Tenderloin Tears

A hard couple of months.
      April he had no roof;
June he was flunked in English
      in twilight time of his senior year
(some years later, a teacher on staff
      telling him to ask the ailing professor
why he did so, only to go too late,
      death claiming him).
Late June, there were the steady knocks
      on his "Tenderloin door" at night,
a 75 cent a day room with bathroom down the hall.
      He would shove the bureau
against the locked door with chair on top.
      July 6, his father died.
It was a spring/summer of loss and isolation.
      Which one the worst reality?
In depth, looking back,
      it was feeling of losing his mother
(his deepest love and in an actual sense,
      his human family).
Later on, tears gushed forth.

Easter Vacation

It was April 8, some Spring in the air,
          but a 17 year old found himself walking Market Street
from 8th and Market to the Ferry Building, back and forth.
          His question, where to spend the night?

He had been given a ride from boarding school,
          arrived at 2415 Octavia Street (at Broadway) a little after 6.
Discovered someone else living where he and his mother lived
          at Christmas time (second floor facing Broadway).
He found a payphone and made one call.
          He was told that his mother lost her job,
the employers not wanting to give benefits to their senior employee.
          There was no offer of sofa to sleep the night
or help to find lodging for the next day.
          Then he walked and walked and walked
up and down San Francisco's Market Street.
          It was getting late. He was tired.
The Bus Depot was on 7th Street, a short turn from Market Street.
          He made a decision, walked in, took tooth brush, wash rag,
towel from the locker that he had rented when he was trying to figure out
          what to do.
Saw a bench with not many people around.
          He felt it safe and dozed off.
In the middle of the night, a man tapped his shoulder and woke him.
          He motioned for him to follow.
He walked towards the 7th Street exit.

He, dazed, half-asleep, stood up, took a few steps.
Then realized that this was not good.

He did not go out of the depot as the man wanted.
He turned and went back to his bench.

The reality was sudden unintended abandonment
which his mother, a great woman as her life shows,
agonized over greatly when she found out about it.

At the time, she didn't know where he was, and he didn't
know where she was.

And no one in-between helped them get together.
He clearly suffered; she suffered more.

What was the nugget in the situation?

Market Street Hotel

He had about $35. Where it came from, he can't remember.
>But taking his luggage from the rented
>locker at the bus depot,

he walked the short way to the decent-looking hotel.
>He went up to the desk, asking the man for
>the cheapest room.

It was $7.00. But the clerk warned that it was next to the
bathroom
>and the elevator. He said, "No problem,"

knowing it better than a bench in the bus depot.
>He stayed there a number of days before the
>"vacation" was over,

and it was time to go back to boarding school.
>He can't recall where he ate or what he did.

Years later when he worked in the Tenderloin, he thought of
        creating a shelter for runaway teenagers.*
He explored getting the money for it, and felt the best approach
        was to seek approval and backing from the
        Tenderloin adults
who, in a sense, "ran things on their level."
        They listened to him, wanted to partner with him,
        but he was against that.
Then the leader said,
        "Okay, we'll let you do it.
        Do you know why?
He paused.
        "Because you know the feeling."

* The Center did not "get off the ground," but he tried.

41

Cursing

His mother taught him not to curse.
     When living alone in the Tenderloin at 17,
looking 15 he was told,
     he would go out of his 75 cent a day room
(with bathroom down the hall),
     and walk and walk and walk,
taking in well-known foul language
     which he did not repeat.
He never cursed in that environment,
     nor in any other,
not even in twilight time.
     His single parent mother who was poor,
had no high school or values instruction
     (no father, mother died when she was 9),
did what many others couldn't.

A Mother's Deep Love

Tenderloin teen, 17, sudden mother loss (April 8),
    father death (July 6),
lack of money the cause of each,
    creating emptiness never to be erased.
His father he hardly knew, having been separated
    when he was five, but the unhardened youth
wanted to see where he lived.
    The manager of the 16th Street Hotel
showed him his father's room, scant belongings
    and painful reminders of what happens
when a mean man living on the same floor
    ties up the bathroom so others cannot use.
He could only speculate that was why his father rushed
    from his dwelling to go to the bathroom at the bar
across the street where he worked, a car hitting him
    as he left the curb.

It was a summer to remember. Adults didn't know who he was,
    didn't hear or see him. He was poor, isolated,
    with great losses, no visible substantial support,
    neither financial
    nor emotional.
His guiding goal, to help those who entered his life.
    Those months were against him.
How did he get through the pain points
    (and future hurdles which were to come)?
It was his mother's Deep Love,
    though she was not a touch away.

STREETS THAT DO HAVE ENOUGH

WAKING STREETS

Poetic Questions?

Poets, spirits of imagination,
  do not draw swords,
nor add to mankind's misery,
  just normal souls,
or are they?
  How much unselfish ink
in their creative pen?
  What makes them content?
How many challenge their perceptions?
  How many are in harmony
with their core?
  How many cry with joy
when finishing words that sing?

Amos Alonzo Stagg

Legendary Football Coach
1862-1965 (102 years)

I met him when he was 99,
      asked like so many others,
"What is the secret of your longevity?
      He said
that he was an athlete
      with all the activity that goes with it.
And as a coach (football, basketball, baseball),
      he never asked his players
to do some laps
      that he did not do with them.
After retirement, he continued exercising.

Suffering

Suffering is a teacher,
       but what a way to learn.
To be grateful though
       when the price is right.

Guides

Courage in cracks,
       strength in pebbles,
sea carpeting shore,
       stream that flows,
star that sparkles,
       garden after watering,
flat stone on which to step,
       candle flame that waves,
"typewriter" enabling,
       eraser's noble task,
dawn's freshness,
       sun's shadows,
night's inspiration,
       maps for the journey.

Ego

An ill-bred remark,
        rude glance,
mean slight,
        words that hurt deeply,
ego not understanding
        the sacred moment.

To Young Adults

HOW MANY

enjoy what they have,
see the nugget in the situation,

look at the bright side regularly,
realize time is short,

understand little things can be big,
know life has numerous new beginnings,

feel that "winter" comes down to
         health, family, love, and money?

Wanting It

They said I couldn't and I did,
  my efforts perhaps not to soar,
but I rose above
  because I wanted it more.

Unmet Relationships

Have you thought of unmet relationships,
    those that might have flowed
had paths met?
    Time glided on unknowing steps,
baffling fate challenged an encounter,
    what would have happened
we'll never know, perhaps at times
    to travel into wonder and regret.

Shining Moments

Eyeing white rose in broken vase,
       sturdy age of tree's rugged bark,
fearless birds flying over raging waters.

In winter memories of parents,
       smiling three year old saying
"I love you too."

Writing poem which touches soul,
       depth feeling that you are loved
for what you are.

Spring

May you gather March flowers,
      colorful art of Spring,
see spirituality in buds unfolding,
      each dawn, another hope.
May you gaze intently at tender leaves
      and watch them sway in the breeze.
May you dance in your garden,
      being very much You at what you do.
May you seek and find healthy peace
      amid unsympathetic noise,
train self to reset no matter what,
      core self-talk
to guide tranquil mind and sacred steps
      towards becoming
the best possible person.

A Poet

What is the chief trait of a poet?
      Is it imagination?
One would think so.
      But what is behind imagination?
Is it curiosity, study, experience, meditation?
      What part mind, heart, soul?
Friends, parents, ancestors?
      Nature, dreams, gentle art, love voice?
Likely everything, and having read
      so many poor poems.

"Failures"

"Failures" who kept on going...to success:
ABRAHAM LINCOLN 1809-1865,
THOMAS EDISON 1847-1931,
BENJAMIN FRANKLIN 1706-1790,
LEO TOLSTOY 1828-1910,
    author of *War and Peace*,
OLIVER GOLDSMITH 1728-1774,
    author of *The Vicar of Wakefield*,
WILLIAM MAKEPEACE THACKERAY 1811-1863,
    author of *Vanity Fair*,
SAMUEL JOHNSON 1709-1784,
    author of *A Dictionary of the English Language*,
and many 21st century spirits who haven't quit,
    not allowing the sword of "failure"
to cut into their courage, fire, and persistence,
    but continue to make the most of what they are doing.

Fragile Child

Despite high hurdles, burned beans,
    soggy toast, wrong road signs,
friends who disappoint,
    enemies who don't,
never to know
    where human spirit might have gone
had he or she
    taken one small step farther.

WINDING STREETS

Evil Ways

What is the content of those
      who sow discord?
The Old Testament's
      Book of Proverbs*
speaks strongly
      against one who does.

Do those who do
      destroy threads in someone's garment
and lessen precious minutes,
      or, do they create a patch
for others to weave someday?
      Or both?

cf. Proverbs 6:16-19
King James Version

Calm Surroundings

Life's music speaking to the soul,
      chanting a tranquil psalm,
single steps advancing gracefully,
      surrounding self with soothing calm.

At home in therapeutic garden
      with flowers grown to share,
not so much success to declare,
      but vigilant, reverential care.

Sidewalk spirituality, wellness,
      taking it easy in an ordeal,
being awake and mindful,
      doing one's best with wise zeal.

Blessed

Two unique spirits,
       mantled goodness
for another's magnified glass,
       whispering to each other
on blended marble,
       polished pebbles,
dusty trails,
       streams with sacred silence,
content in misty rain,
       ocean, wind, burning sun,
cheerful fire, sheltering rock,
       birds resting on yule logs,
playful fish moving in life-giving waters,
       humble spirituality all-embracing,
unveiling in the depth of their souls,
       an irreplaceable word
in life's continued whirlpool, Love,
       "Love is the soul of genius,"*
and what greater beauty
       than to be loved
for what one is!

Attributed to Wolfgang Amadeus Mozart

The Sea 101

We all get old,
              except the sea.
We all get tired,
              except the sea.
It accepts totally: that's the key.
              Why not me?

SPACIOUS STREETS

"Glady"

108 years (near 109), d. 2/14/2018
The doctor said
she suffered from "TMB."
Too Many Birthdays.

Asked how did she live so long,
she responded lightly,
"coffee, hard-boiled eggs,
peanut butter."

Don'ts

Don't look back,
        don't fight their system,
don't say their attitude is bad,
        live each day as well as you can.

Tale of life,
        all give, no get,
learn to be still, alert, wise,
        especially when the rocks are rolling.

Musing

We do more good than we realize
    with less control than we think,
might wonder about precious moments we miss,
    some feelings perhaps that
ascetic ways at times can make one more aware,
    IF
    steps are in harmony with one's core,
    human suffering doesn't overwhelm,
    one isn't embittered by fate,
    and one has had at least one great love,
not failing to try to be conscious
    of reach and steps.

Heart of the Hill

Is the flower
        the heart of the hill,
or is it the trail
        with its secret destination?

"Wasted Years"

Were the "wasted years" wasted,
      meaningless reality
at prime time when energy and drive
      were willing and ready for that age?
Did that period motivate me
      to use this precious time well,
give me strength for deeper understanding,
      suffering which will benefit others
          somehow?

Seashore

Do you have grateful feelings
  eyeing white-capped waves,
smooth sand dollars,
  artistic seaweed?
Do they touch an attentive heart?
  Do you feel
when they say the least,
  the greater the art?

Birthday

At 62 she wrote Health, Education & Welfare,
        May 25, 1956, to find out what was her correct age;
Chicago fire burnt the original records.
        Her mother died when she was nine.
She never knew her father.
        She was not sure.

She lived to 74 or 75, never finding out which.

        Many are asked how old they are.
They answer or are silent.
        She was never positive
of what most others clearly know.

Lavender Rose

Lavender rose,
      tender symbol in soul-expanding sun,
elegant emblem blossoming colorfully
      above earth's mosaic floor,
looking up, looking down,
      looking in, looking out,
calling out mystically
      putting forth silent speech,
gazing intently at
      clustering flowerets,
radiant at morn,
      art form at evening tide,
glowing in favorite green,
      branching amorous
even in foggy air,
      painted dream,
ever-beating heart
      in sunny garden,
enlightening
      whomever near.

Distraction

A good man,
      solid know-how worker,
his tool on that day,
      a hand-held circular saw.
30 years, no problem,
      then,
left arm reached too far,
      3 surgeries did not heal.

Did his mind wander
      in midst of movement
he knew well,
      concentration taking a stroll,
metal having no mercy?

He was focusing on a task
      he had controlled many times.
How important deep inner sureness
      and being in the present!

Magic Words

Magic in ***prioritizing***,
         clarifies steps,
allows energy to rise.

If absurdity peaks its head,
         to ***breathe*** in and out,
30 seconds of calm,

perhaps think of the day's
         little joys, if you can,
but the main thing...***work***,
         and the might of it.

One Friend

When pillars shake,
　　　　life at low tide,
we all need one friend
　　　　to be at our side.

Cheerful at Age 100

Learned email at 90,
independently living at age 100,
could walk up stairs,
cook for self,
boil eggs,
make oatmeal.
Had lived in her house
for 70 years, then
her caring grandson
moved her to a residence
with the lowest level of care,
no more stairs to climb,
and she lost that ability, yet
continually engaged,
never let darkness take over,
was always cheerful,
with a smile
and a bit of humor
shining through in her words,
"Who's that old lady in the mirror?"

Art

Art, music to the soul,
　　　　a conversation, painting, poem,
bird on limb,
　　　　tree waving in wind,
father throwing ball to his child,
　　　　10 year old saying, "I love you too,"
fallible human having a great day.

Content of the Person

When Spirit tends to lead to new places,
       there are those who can get you down
if you let them,
       if they do, that's LIFE.
People don't read humans well,
       too many mental mirrors,
rumbling thoughts
       that disorient still mind.
At times take in words
       that they don't understand,
judge without accurate edge.
       The world turns with a multitude of spirits
indifferent to plight of the common person,
       while great souls breathe on lawn, in alleys,
on shore, ships, dry land, damp desert.
       They know it's what you are that counts.

Grunt Work

We all have had grunt work,
      sink, dishes, closet, trunk,
tackling accumulation,
      storage that always needs work,
trying tasks,
      shadowed minutes,
are they always lost time?
      are creative seeds in there somewhere?
do they contribute to limitless imagination?
      Why don't we get it?

Stories

Where have all the stories gone,
      to sky ceiling, ocean bottom?
What made people forget
      after they listened with attentive eyes?

Many surface, but some not intact,
      strange journey in certain ways,
twists and turns, slants, biases, omissions.
      Why?   Is it taking in too much sugar?

His Stay, 96 Years

His family line ending,
      few belongings,
penned nothing,
      no legacy.
Lived the virtues extraordinaire,
      especially compassion.
Became known nationally
      and internationally
in his field.
      His life-long goal,
just wanted to help those
      who entered his life.

Ode to a Ten Year Old

I'm incomplete without you,
      in my soul there you are.
I never learned to be in a family,
      nor had one to share my years,
now to push each of these aside,
      because I love you number one,
my surrogate grandson.

SILENT STREETS

What a Blessing

What a blessing it is
        to have understanding eyes
and a loving heart!

What Gift?

What secret gift do I leave on planet stay?
        Hidden kindnesses?
Great intent? Truth in soul?
        Accepting the thunder?
Meditating no matter what?
        Remote belonging
which touches deep?

A Little Bit is Big

In those days, 6% of youth went to high school,
        but study she did,
was just about always cheerful,
        looking at the bright side,
liked to encourage those with good goals
        to go a wee bit further,
her favorite saying,
        "A little bit added to a little bit
makes a little bit more."

"How Many...?"

How many pray for those who have much less,
      or who know the feeling of living without true family,
silent phone, personal mail rare, no car to drive,
      too many potatoes, beans on payday?

How many pray for saintly strangers,
      some with masks, veils, aprons, attache cases,
others fighting blank isolation, serious losses, lonely nights,
      voices whispering brokenly reaching for hope.

How many pray for those without conscience,
      who have done dark things
and will not stop, until the last days
      when guilt takes mental stage?

Meditation

So many times my meditation was not love.
        It was thoughts, feelings, hopes for the day.
Sometimes searching silence for a nugget,
        instead of swift arrows going through
wise, undemanding love
        for those who enter my life
during 15 or 16 waking hours.
        It is only then
that I can truly feel my soul.

They Said He'd Never…

They flunked him in his senior year,
       high school a five year run,
with no diploma offered.
       Nor did he collect a college degree.
It was said he would never go to graduate school.

He went 10 years to graduate schools,
       completing 4 graduate studies' programs,
including a 1-year European Diploma, enduring
       the loss of not getting another degree
with a 3.6 GPA, old transcripts frowned upon, also
       delving into instructive, private study 40+ years.

He held two Life Teaching Credentials
       and had a third which expired.
Some years later, a former teacher took him aside
       at an alumni gathering, saying,
"We just didn't see you. We missed you."

ABOUT THE AUTHOR

CHARLES HOLMES writes to touch people's lives, He has written three life-reflecting adult poetry books, *Reflections of the Heart* and *Reflections of the Soul* that offer meditative thoughts for quiet consideration, and *Streets That Speak* that touches upon some realities of streets that do not have enough, and streets that do have enough. He also has compiled rich common sense in *Thoughts From Millie*, which is the result of many interviews when she was 89, 90, and 91 years old.

He has written eight children's books (page vi). Some are fun; others, sort of "cool." Still others are on the serious side.

He has created three recreation centers for children, has taught at two universities and one community college, has done social work with the elderly poor, and has authored two studies about their difficulties. He has delved into the magic of study formally and privately for many years.

He is a surrogate grandfather for 10 year old Aidan, grandson in heart.

Aidan Lee Elenteny, grandson in heart,
and
Charles Holmes

ACKNOWLEDGEMENTS

Joan Arnott

Barbara Elenteny

Sheila Helms

Nadia McCaffrey

Rev. Bill McDonald

MeMe Riordan

TO CONTACT THE AUTHOR

please email
rlg121212@gmail.com

Made in the USA
Columbia, SC
07 September 2019